Safe Proficient Motoring® is for both new and experienced drivers' alike.

The modules have been designed to give you the detailed information you need in a simple and straightforward way and link together to form a comprehensive learning journey.

Each unit contains instructions and diagrams plus '**SPM** tips' to help you learn how to drive safely. You will also find extra information in the appendix if you need it.

These modules are NOT designed as a sole method for learning 'How to drive' and you should understand that driving is also a 'practical' subject.

Therefore, the information in the modules should be used, in addition to some other form of guidance and practice e.g. having lessons with a fully qualified Approved Driving Instructor – DSA A.D.I. (Car), family member or friend. (see SPM Tip below)

If you like what you read and learn then please let others know.

Good luck and safe driving

"Learn to Drive, without being in a Car™**"**

SPM Tip-
Highway code 2011 page 123- To accompany a Learner Driver YOU must be at least 21 years old AND hold a full valid car driving licence for 3 years+

Published by Safe Proficient Motoring

Contents

Unit 1.1 Safety Checks   4

Unit 1.2 Foot Controls   6

Unit 1.3 Hand Controls   8

Unit 1.4 Moving Off   16

Unit 1.5 Normal Stops   18

Unit 1.6 Left Turns   20

Unit 1.7 Right Turns   23

Appendix   27-32

SPM tip-
Highway code 2011 Rule 99 page 31-32
YOU must make sure anyone
under 14 years old wears a seat belt
– it's the law

When you get into a car you must do the "SAFETY CHECKS" These checks used to be called the "COCKPIT DRILL".

Safety Checks

The first check we must make is the **DOOR(s)**.

This is to make sure our door is shut properly We don't want to fall out of the car or have our door hit anything *Appendix 1

Next is the **SEAT**

You need to reach the left pedal by your feet AND press it fully to the floor

Next adjust your backrest so that you can reach the steering wheel

Finally we check that the **HEAD RESTRAINT** is positioned behind our head
* Appendix 1

Then check **MIRROR(s)**.

The mirror on the left near to the kerb is the **NEARSIDE** mirror.

The mirror on the right, the drivers side, is the **OFFSIDE** mirror.

These two mirrors are known as the **EXTERIOR DOOR/SIDE MIRRORS**.

The third mirror is the **INTERIOR REAR VIEW** mirror.
This gives us a view to the rear of the car *Appendix 1+2

The fourth check is our **SEAT BELT**.

This may be the 1st time you will sit in the driver seat So putting your seat belt on from the **RIGHT** may feel a little strange to begin with but don't worry you get used to it.

To put your seat belt on properly you reach across your body with your **LEFT** hand and pull the seat belt out, keeping hold of the clip.

Then place your **RIGHT** arm through the seat belt, still keeping hold of the clip with your **LEFT** hand.

With your **RIGHT** hand **PULL** out the seat belt, **BUT** make sure that you have your palm facing **UPWARDS** with your **THUMB UNDER** the seat belt so that it is not twisted.

Now pull the seat belt out with your **RIGHT** hand to allow the seat belt clip to reach the holder on your left, next to your seat and clip it in with your **LEFT** hand. Then make sure that the seat belt is resting **FLAT** across your chest and your lap.

There are SIX safety checks. I will deal with the first 4 now & the other 2 later after the handbrake

Safety Checks

Accelerator
Also known as:
Gas, Revs, Power

Brake

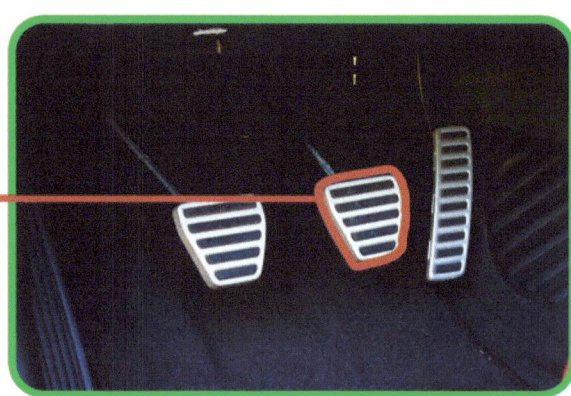

Clutch

There are 3 pedals in the 'footwell'

Foot Controls

The RIGHT pedal is the ACCELERATOR.

We use our RIGHT FOOT ONLY for this pedal.

It is sometimes called the GAS, REVS or POWER.

It CONTROLS THE FLOW OF FUEL, FROM THE FUEL TANK TO THE ENGINE and works like a tap.

The more you press the pedal the more the fuel flows. Also the OPPOSITE applies, the less you press the pedal the less fuel flows.

Then the engine produces more or less power depending on the amount we press * Appendix 3

The MIDDLE pedal is the FOOTBRAKE.

Again we use our RIGHT FOOT. This is because we don't want to be accelerating AND braking at the same time.

The footbrake applies EQUAL PRESSURE AT THE SAME TIME TO ALL FOUR WHEELS, slowing the car down smoothly and evenly.

Try to brake gently but firmly over a period of time. This is called 'PROGRESSIVE' braking.

Brake gently and firmly because hard or harsh braking could cause you to lose control or the car could skid and you may even have an accident! It takes practise so keep it SAFE.

The LEFT pedal is the CLUTCH.

You use your LEFT FOOT ONLY for this pedal.

This is because the clutch does several important jobs so we want to devote our left foot to it. Now keeping it simple, the clutch is a separating device.

It is made up of TWO plates. One plate is attached to the engine and when the engine is switched on, it turns continuously, unless we run out of petrol, turn the engine off or stall the car.

The other plate is attached to the gearbox through to the wheels which drive the car *Appendix 3

There are 3 pedals in the 'footwell'

Foot Controls

Gears

The gear lever is between the 2 front seats in front of the handbrake and is made up of the gear knob and lever (see diagram) There are 5 forward gears and one reverse. For now we are just dealing with the forward gears.

1st gear is used to move off and for slow manoeuvring of the car, 2nd, 3rd and 4th gear are used to build up our speed and 5th gear is our cruising gear for when we get above 40mph. I want to concentrate on the first 4 gears for now.

They form the shape of a capital letter 'H' and we find 1st ,3rd and 5th gears at the front of the gearbox and 2nd and 4th gears at the back. Neutral is 'No gear', it is where the gear lever rests when the car is not being used. Usually Neutral is found between 3rd and 4th gears. Most gearboxes are 'spring' loaded and this means that the gear lever will remain between 3rd and 4th until it is pushed against the spring

Neutral

 1st gear push LEFT and then FORWARDS

 2nd gear push LEFT and then BACKWARDS

 3rd gear just push FORWARDS

 4th gear just push BACKWARDS

Most people find the gear change from 2nd to 3rd is the trickiest!
SPM Tip -
Hold the top of the gear knob gently and ease forward allowing the spring to take the lever to the original N position THEN push forwards for 3rd (practice it with the engine off – but remember to dis-engage the clutch, It is sometimes suggested to 'palm' the gear lever BUT this means you do not have as much control as if you hold it and also you cannot feel the shape of the 'H'

Button on Handbrake

Handbrake

The handbrake is a lever device and is either on or off.
When the lever is up as in the diagram the handbrake is ON

To release the handbrake you first need to pull it up slightly and then depress the button at the end of the handbrake lever to allow the handbrake to be lowered down and taken off

The handbrake on most modern cars ONLY works on the REAR two wheels. Therefore, only use the handbrake once the vehicle is stopped BUT, remember to press in the button BEFORE you apply the handbrake to prevent unnecessary wear and tear!

Once the handbrake is up and firmly on you release the button

If you want to slow down or stop use the footbrake because this works on ALL 4 wheels and the handbrake only works on two

Now we have covered the Handbrake and Gears we must finish the Safety Checks- Remember there are 6

The 5th and 6th Safety Checks are HANDBRAKE and NEUTRAL and are sometimes known as the 'pre-starting' checks

We should do them in this order to check it is Safe for us to start our engine, The reason is that if we checked Neutral before our Handbrake and did not realise the Handbrake was not on properly or had come off then our car could begin to move!

Our engine would not be on, which usually means, because most cars have 'power assisted brakes', our brakes may not work properly.
This may be, potentially dangerous!

So remember Handbrake BEFORE Neutral

This means that the six Safety Checks are

Door, Seat, Mirror, Seat Belt, Handbrake, Neutral

OR TRY THIS

Don't | Start | Moving | Safety 1st | Happy | Now

(DSMSHN)

SPM Tip -
IF YOU DRIVE THE SAME CAR EVERYDAY
THEN YOUR SEAT AND MIRRORS
SHOULD NOT NEED ADJUSTING

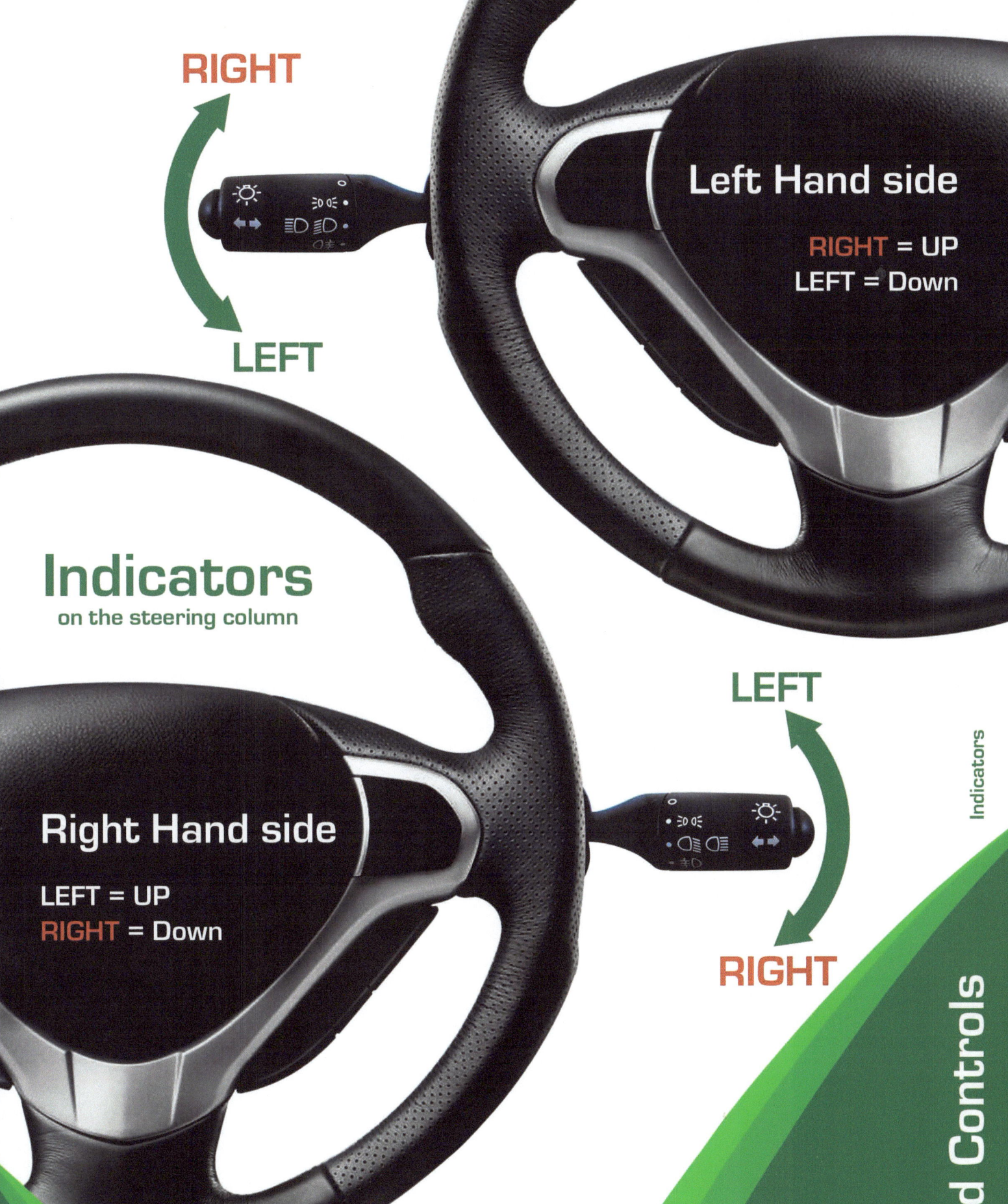

Indicators
on the steering column

Left Hand side
RIGHT = UP
LEFT = Down

Right Hand side
LEFT = UP
RIGHT = Down

Hand Controls

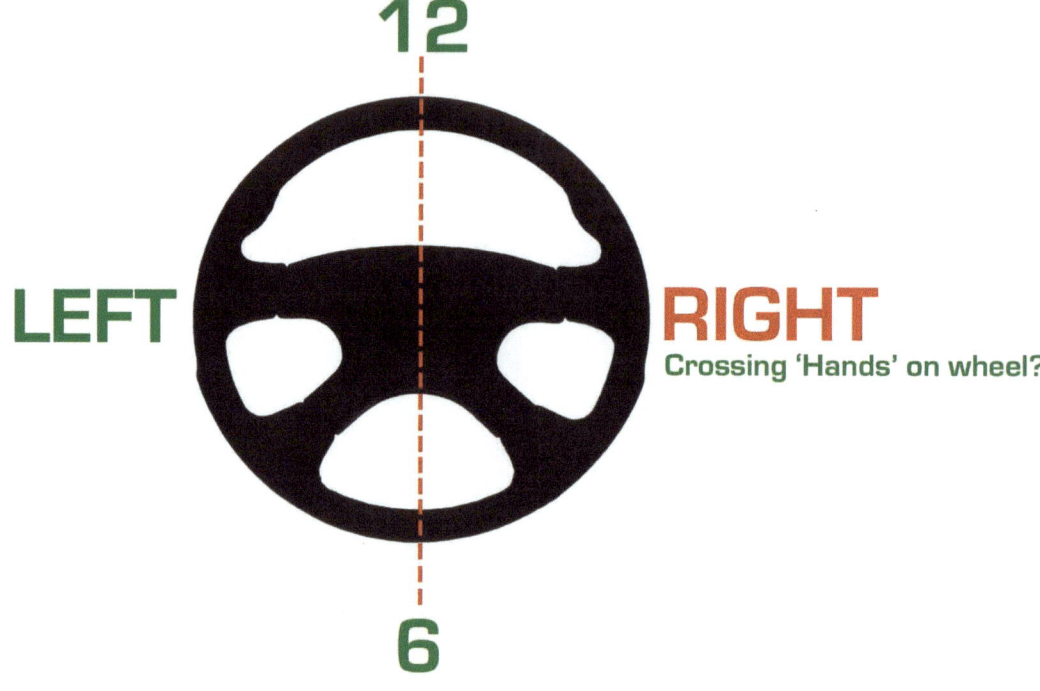

12

LEFT　　　　　RIGHT

Crossing 'Hands' on wheel?

6

10 Hands at Ten and Two **2**

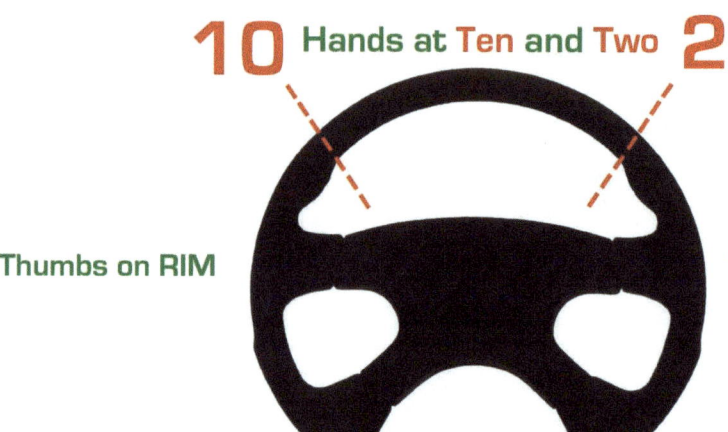

Thumbs on RIM　　　　Turn wheel through 'LOCK'

Steering

Pull & Push method of Steering

Left	Right
PULL - LEFT	PULL – RIGHT
PUSH - Right	PUSH – Left

PULL – Down
PUSH - Up

Hand Controls

12

Think of the steering wheel like a clock, with 12 at the top and 6 at the bottom, this divides the wheel vertically in half...

The Left hand stays on the left side while
the Right hand stays on the right

This way we avoid 'crossing our ARMS' on the wheel, which is always wrongly referred to as crossing your 'hands'.
If you keep your left hand on the left and your right hand on the right, then you will not pass past 12 or 6 on the clock face and will keep both your hands and arms from being crossed

When we steer we turn the wheel to create the steering 'lock'
Don't grip the wheel, but rest your thumbs against the rim of the wheel, so they are NOT tucked in. Otherwise, when you steer properly, you would hit your thumb against the inner sections of the wheel, which really can hurt, trust me I did it once...

When we drive we hold the wheel at "Ten to Two" on the clock,
To steer correctly and safely we should use the PULL & PUSH method.
A tip to remember is that whichever way you are turning is
the hand you PULL with e.g. Left turn PULL with your LEFT hand.
After you pull you would then PUSH with your right hand

The trick to master is that your hands should always be opposite each other like a mirror image

As you pull DOWN with one hand the other hand SLIDES down the wheel to meet at the 6 position

You then PUSH up with the hand you slid while you slide the original hand back up to the top of the wheel at 12

Try to work your hands from 12 to 6 - that is top to bottom, to maximise both your steering and your control
Sorry if it sounds confusing but it does take practice..

Hopefully the notes opposite and on the following 2 pages will help

Steering

Hand Controls

STEERING LEFT

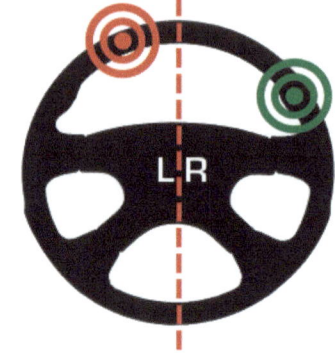

LEFT HAND

RIGHT HAND

Grip wheel at 12 o'clock and PULL DOWN to 6

SLIDE DOWN wheel to 6

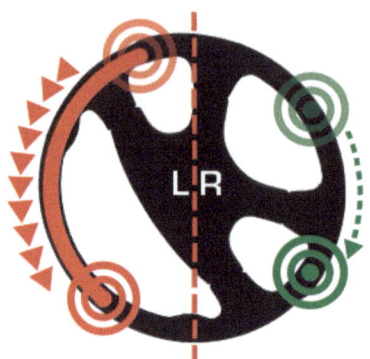

SLIDE UP wheel to 12

Grip wheel and PUSH UP to 12

Grip wheel at 12 o'clock and PULL DOWN to 6

SLIDE DOWN wheel to 6

STEERING RIGHT

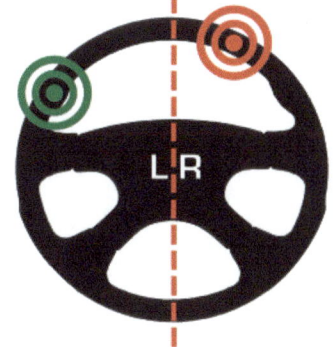

LEFT HAND   **RIGHT HAND**

SLIDE DOWN wheel to 6   Grip wheel at 12 o'clock and **PULL DOWN** to 6

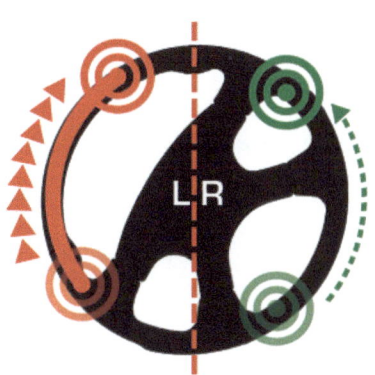

Grip wheel and **PUSH UP** to 12   **SLIDE UP** wheel to 12

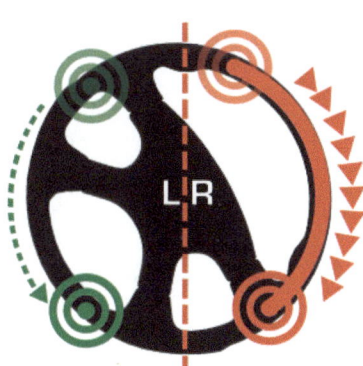

SLIDE DOWN wheel to 6   Grip wheel at 12 o'clock and **PULL DOWN** to 6

Steering

Hand Controls

Moving Off

Mirror, Signal, Manoeuvre

Set ACC to 'Lively Hum' - (1 inch)

Clutch to FLOOR & Select 1st Gear

Slowly release Clutch "Bite"
(Engine noise changes)

KEEP BOTH FEET STILL

Left shoulder - (Pavement)

MSM
- **Mirror** & Front
- **Signal** Right? (if necessary)
- **Manoeuvre** – Right shoulder

'100%' safe (blind Spots) [Your Head]

Look forward & release Handbrake

Car moves [if NOT Clutch UP £1 coin]

KEEP BOTH FEET STILL

Walking Pace -
Release Clutch gently & fully [foot away]

Control speed with Acc &/or Brake

Cancel Signal (if used)

Remember to STEER

To move off we use the 'MSM' routine – Mirror, Signal, Manoeuvre

First set your Accelerator to a 'lively hum' (press about 1inch/2-3cm)

Using your left foot press Clutch to the floor and select 1st gear (move gear lever Left and Forward) Slowly begin to release your clutch to find the 'bite' (engine noise changes to a steady tone)

KEEP BOTH FEET STILL while you check it is safe to go. 1st check over your Left shoulder to make sure there are no pedestrians or cyclists on your nearside

Then check your rear view Mirror & in front to see if you need to Signal, if you do then signal Right - page 11

Finally look over your Right Shoulder to make sure it is 100% Safe before you Manoeuvre Off
(this also means you have checked your natural 'Blind Spot' created by YOUR HEAD between the rear view and offside mirrors)

Look forward and release the Handbrake.

The car should begin to move
(if it doesn't then release your CLUTCH slightly about the thickness of a £1 coin to help the car move)

Once the car moves KEEP BOTH FEET STILL

This gives the Clutch plates chance to line up correctly so you move off smoothly & safely under control

When the car reaches about a 'walking pace; then slowly release the clutch fully and gently and take your foot away

Then control your speed with the Acc or Brake

Cancel your Right signal (if used)

and Finally – remember to STEER

Before Moving Off check:

1. LEFT Shoulder (Pavement)
2. In front
3. Rear View MIRROR
4. RIGHT Shoulder (Blind Spot)

Remember to be SAFE 100% SAFE

Normal Stops - SAFE, LAWFUL, CONVENIENT

Safe - _____?_____

Lawful - _____?_____

Convenient - _____?_____

MSM {
- **Mirror** & front
- **Signal** Left (if necessary)
- **Manoeuvre** – Off Acc onto Brake to Stop

Just before Stop (1 Metre/3-4 feet) Clutch quickly to FLOOR [Stall]

KEEP BOTH FEET STILL

Apply Handbrake

Select Neutral

Relax Feet

Cancel Signal (if used)

Normal Stops - SAFE, LAWFUL, CONVENIENT

Normal Stops are not as tricky as Moving Off

First we must choose a place for us to stop

It must be Safe, Lawful and Convenient

Safe = e.g. No bends or bridges

Lawful = Not on yellow lines or where parking restrictions apply

Convenient = Not blocking entrances or driveways etc.

We use the MSM routine again to stop Mirror Signal Manoeuvre

First, check your rear view Mirror to make sure it is safe to stop, then you will know if you need to Signal, if you do, signal Left - page 11

Finally, we Manoeuvre by gradually releasing the accelerator and then braking gently to slow down and stop (use Right foot)

Just BEFORE you stop, about 1 metre/3-4 feet, you must quickly press your Clutch, with your Left foot, fully to the floor

Then KEEP BOTH FEET STILL

Next apply your Handbrake and select Neutral
You can the relax your feet and cancel your signal, if used

It is important to apply the Handbrake BEFORE selecting Neutral, this is because when you have stopped, you need to make the car secure by locking the wheels with the handbrake

If you do your gears first, then should you be hit from behind for any reason, your car will travel forwards more and could put you in danger, especially at junctions

Remember be SAFE, 100% SAFE

Mirror, Signal, Position, Speed, Look
(MSPSL)

When you come to a left turn the first thing you do is to check your rear view MIRROR to see what is behind you.

We will assume it is safe. If it is not this will be explained in module 2 unit 2.2

Mirror

Next you would SIGNAL left
see INDICATORS in HAND CONTROLS - page 11

Signal

Mirror, Signal, Position, Speed, Look (MSPSL)

Left Turns

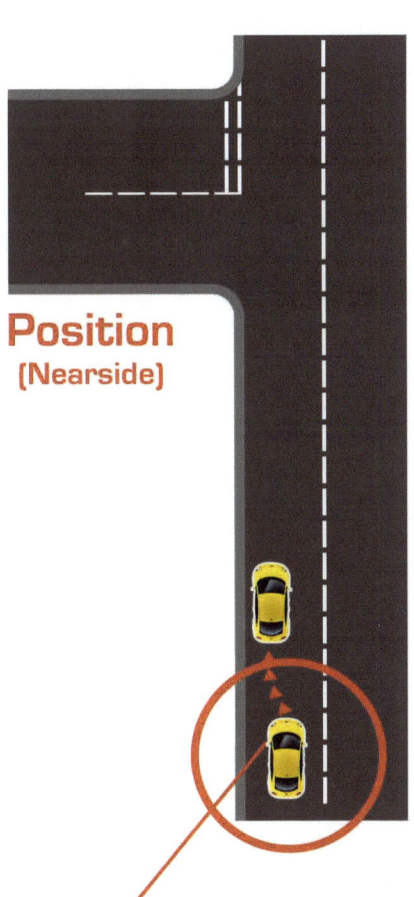

Position
(Nearside)

You must then get the correct position. For left turns that means being nicely in to the left, but not with you're wheels' 'bouncing' through all the drains!

Now before we POSITION ourselves we must check our nearside mirror to ensure there is no danger to our left, for example, from pedestrians or cyclists.

The next step is to control our SPEED so that we can turn the corner safely and under control. Many people struggle with this for many lessons. But I want you to imagine that you could RUN around the corner, then you can take the car around at that same speed i.e. Running Speed. That is about 10-12 mph.

Now you will see some people going around corners faster than that but to be SAFE you must learn to keep your speed at junctions reasonable and controlled

The correct gear for that speed is 2nd gear.

WHEN we change gear is also very important. I want you to try and change gear about 2 or 3 car lengths away from the turn. That's right imagining 2 or 3 car lengths in you mind*Appendix 5

BEFORE we slow our car down to our Running Speed we must look again in our Rear View Mirror to ensure that it is safe for us to slow down

(see Module 2 unit 2.2)

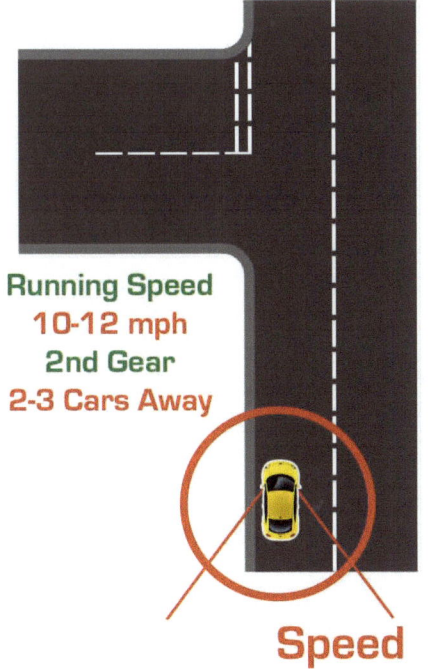

Running Speed
10-12 mph
2nd Gear
2-3 Cars Away

Speed

Mirror, Signal, Position, Speed, Look (MSPSL)

Left Turns

INDUCE BECKON 100% SAFE

Look

Finally we must **LOOK** to see if it is **100% SAFE**, No More and No Less. If it is then we must turn left. Aiming to keep our **POSITION** before, during and after the turn.

We must not swing out before we turn left because if there was an approaching vehicle we may have an accident.

Nor must we lose position during or after the turn because of traffic at the junction.

Again, once we have straightened our vehicle we must check our **REAR VIEW MIRROR** to make sure that it is safe behind for us to drive on. If it is not then we can deal with any danger immediately. Module 2 Unit 2.2

ON THE PAVEMENT

INDUCE BECKON

STOP HERE

Look

That is what we do if the junction is **100% SAFE**. On another occasion we may find some danger at the junction before we turn e.g. a pedestrian crossing the road. If there is any danger we **MUST STOP**. Let the danger clear and then, using first gear, drive on.

If, however the pedestrian is standing **ON THE PAVEMENT** then we **DO NOT STOP**. We do not ignore the pedestrian though, but we do not stop for them either. They are quite safe on the pavement, we cannot control other traffic, so leave them there and drive on.

This way we avoid **TWO** things.

The first is **INDUCING**.
Inducing means to slow down your vehicle and let the pedestrian think it is for them.

The second is **BECKONING**.
Beckoning is if you flash your headlights, wave your hand, shout or whistle.

If the pedestrian is on the pavement leave them there and keep going.

That is how we do left turns **PROPERLY**.

Mirror, Signal, Position, Speed, Look (MSPSL)

Left Turns

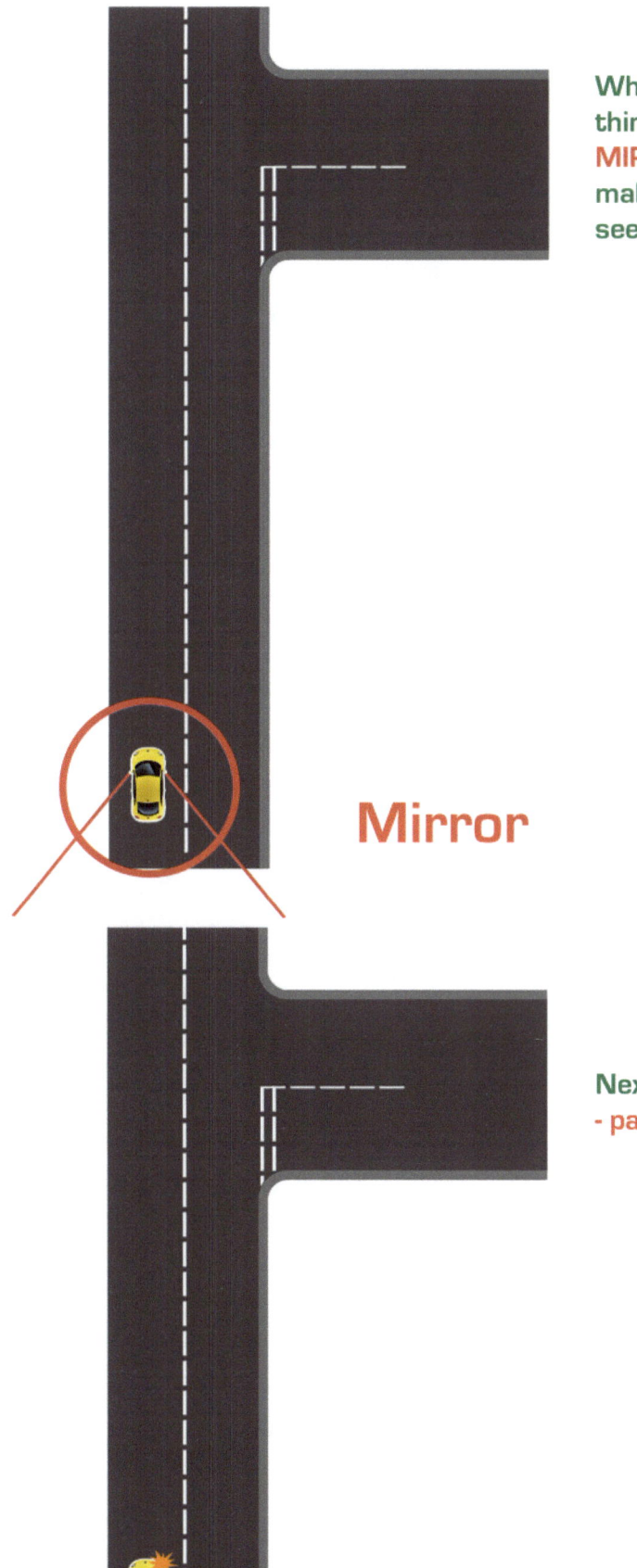

When you come to a right turn the first thing you do is to check your rear view **MIRROR** to see what is behind you and make sure it is **SAFE**
see Module 2 unit 2.2

Mirror

Next you would **SIGNAL** Right
- page 11

Signal

Mirror, Signal, Position, Speed, Look (MSPSL)

Right Turns

You must then get the correct **POSITION**. For right turns that means being over towards the centre white line, but **NOT** over it! Now before we position ourselves we must check our offside mirror to ensure there is no danger to our right, for example, from other vehicles or motorcycles overtaking us.

Position

Offside

The next step is to control our **SPEED** so that we can turn the corner safely and under control. Again I want you to imagine that you could RUN around the corner. That is about 10-12 mph. The correct gear for that speed is 2nd gear. **WHEN**, we change gear is also very important. I want you to try and change gear about 2 or 3 car lengths away from the turn. The same as for left turns* Appendix 5

BEFORE we slow our car down to our Running Speed we must look again in our Rear View Mirror to ensure that it is safe for us to slow down. Module 2 Unit 2.2

Running Speed
10-12 mph
2nd Gear
2-3 Cars Away

Speed

Mirror, Signal, Position, Speed, Look (MSPSL)

Right Turns

Finally we must LOOK to see if it is 100% SAFE, 'No More and No Less'. If it is then we must turn right. Aiming to keep our POSITION before, during and after the turn.

If we were to drift back towards the kerb and there was a vehicle trying to undertake us then we could have an accident! (i.e. car number 1) Also if we were to cut the corner and there was a vehicle approaching the junction then we may again have an accident (see car number 2) So don't cut corners or swerve along the road, stay in position before, during and after the turn. Again, once we have straightened our vehicle we must check our REAR VIEW MIRROR to make sure that it is safe behind for us to drive on. If it is not then we can deal with any danger immediately. Module 2 Unit 2.2

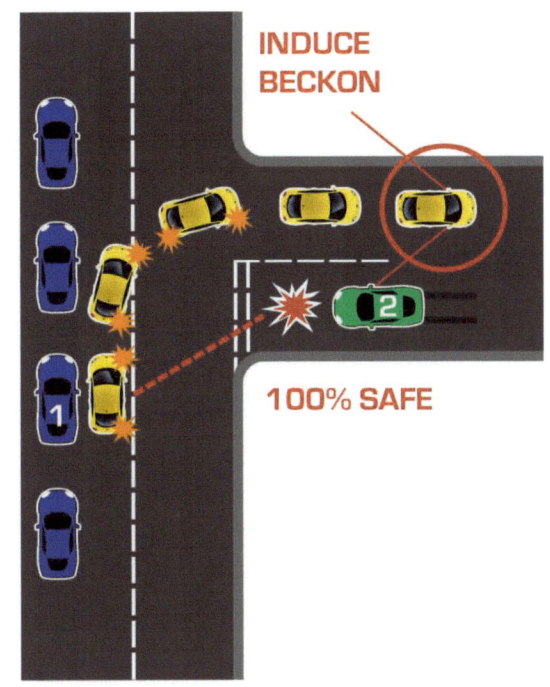

That is what we do if the junction is 100% SAFE. On another occasion we may find some danger at the junction before we turn e.g. a pedestrian crossing the road. If there is any danger we MUST STOP
WHERE DO WE STOP?

We should stop just before the Point of Turn (P.O.T. for short). The POT is defined, as the point opposite where the centre white line of the road we are turning into would meet the centre white line of the road we are on.
If we try and turn right but we have gone past the POT then we will 'Swan Neck' around the corner, which is bad driving and can be dangerous. Also don't turn too soon because you would 'cut' the corner which is also dangerous because of vehicles which maybe approaching the junction

If, however the pedestrian is standing ON THE PAVEMENT then we DO NOT STOP.

We do not ignore the pedestrian though, but we do not stop for them either. They are quite safe on the pavement, we cannot control other traffic, so leave them there and drive on.

Mirror, Signal, Position, Speed, Look (MSPSL)

Right Turns

This way we avoid TWO things. The first is INDUCING the second is BECKONING.

Inducing means to slow down your vehicle and let the pedestrian think it is for them. Beckoning is if you flash your headlights, wave your hand, shout or whistle.

If the pedestrian is on the pavement leave them there and keep going.

Oncoming Traffic

Now the routine for left turns and right turns are the same. However, we all know that with right turns we must deal with 'Oncoming Traffic', which we do not get with left turns!
We must be able to turn right without the approaching traffic having to
SLOW DOWN, SWERVE OR STOP!

If you have very little or no experience on the road then judging this can be very difficult.
So I want you to imagine that you are standing at the P.O.T. (DON'T do it though because you may get run over!)
Now from this point you should be able to WALK, not run, but WALK into the side road, without causing any approaching vehicle to do any of the things we just mentioned above.
Then providing you are in 1st gear and have your 'BITE', then in most cases you can take the car around.

If you are not sure, then wait at the P.O.T. until you are sure it is 100% SAFE.

As we approach the junction though, we will be in 2nd gear, so if you think you could RUN around the corner without affecting the approaching traffic, then keep going, no need to wait at the P.O.T.

That is how we should do right turns PROPERLY.

Remember 100% safe, no more no less!

Mirror, Signal, Position, Speed, Look (MSPSL)

Right Turns

Door

To check your door is shut properly, give the handle a tug to see if the door is secure. Don't pull the door release, as this could cause the door to open and may cause an accident. If you do need to open the door and close it again make sure it is safe before you open it i.e. check there are no other road users near the car!

Seat

You need to adjust your seat so that you can reach the left pedal in the footwell AND press it fully to the floor without stretching or being too close to the steering wheel. Ideally you should have a slight bend in your leg. Next adjust your backrest so that you can easily reach the steering wheel but not be too close for comfort. We don't really want our arms straight or bent right up. Finally we check that the HEAD RESTRAINT on the seat is positioned behind our head with the bottom of the restraint level with our chin. Check with your instructor about how to adjust the seat and head restraint correctly.

Mirrors

Be aware that the interior mirror (rear view) has flat glass, so the view from the rear view mirror is an exact view i.e. if something is 30 feet behind us then it looks 30 feet away in the mirror.

However, with the exterior mirrors, the view we get is diminished i.e. the image we see appears further away than it actually is. This is because the exterior mirrors have curved glass (convex-curves outwards).

The exterior mirrors are curved because it gives us a WIDER FIELD OF VISION. This means that we will get different views form our interior and exterior mirrors.

Get your instructor to help with this. It is something you will get used to in time.

Adjustment of Mirrors Rear view

Try and adjust your interior rear view mirror so that the top of the mirror is horizontal and not crooked and set slightly towards the offside.

You should be able to see your left ear in the right end of the mirror

Exterior

Adjust your exterior mirrors so that, if we imagine the mirror divided vertically into 3 equal parts, the 1st third nearest to the car gives you a view along each side of the car.

Then with the **NEARSIDE** mirror you should see along the pavement at the side of the car in the other two thirds. With the **OFFSIDE** mirror you should be able to see the road to your right in the other two thirds.

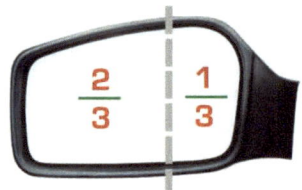 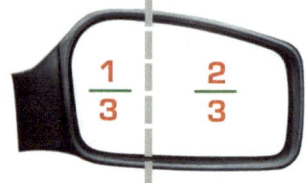

Now it is important to do these checks in the order we have mentioned. That is DOOR, SEAT, MIRROR and SEAT BELT or using the first letter of each word try DSMS

DON'T START MOVING SAFETY 1ST.

Why must we do the Safety Checks in this order?

The reason we must try to do them in this order is, let's say we did the checks in reverse order. Then it would be Safety 1st Moving Start Don't? Which does not make sense. But more importantly, if you put your seat belt on first then adjust your mirrors, when you move your seat you could end up strangling yourself with the seat belt and your mirrors would need doing AGAIN because you have moved your seat AFTER you adjusted them. Plus, because you have not checked your DOOR yet, if it was not closed someone could drive past and hit it.

So you are sat there with **NO DOOR**, being strangled by your seat belt, you cannot see in your mirrors properly and you haven't even started the engine yet!

That is not a great start to your driving experience!
So do them in the order we said each time then you won't have those problems.

Accelerator - We can use the accelerator as a form of brake! That is, if you are driving down the road and see another vehicle ahead doing something you are not sure about, then you can release the pedal, slowing the car down. Then you can re-apply the pressure on the accelerator again when you are sure it is safe.

Clutch - When the clutch is UP the two plates are held TOGETHER by a strong spring (see diagram below) This is known as ENGAGED. When you press the clutch DOWN the two plates are pushed APART against the spring (hence the pressure under your foot). This is known as DIS-ENGAGED.

So UP is ENGAGED (together), DOWN is DIS-ENGAGED (apart).

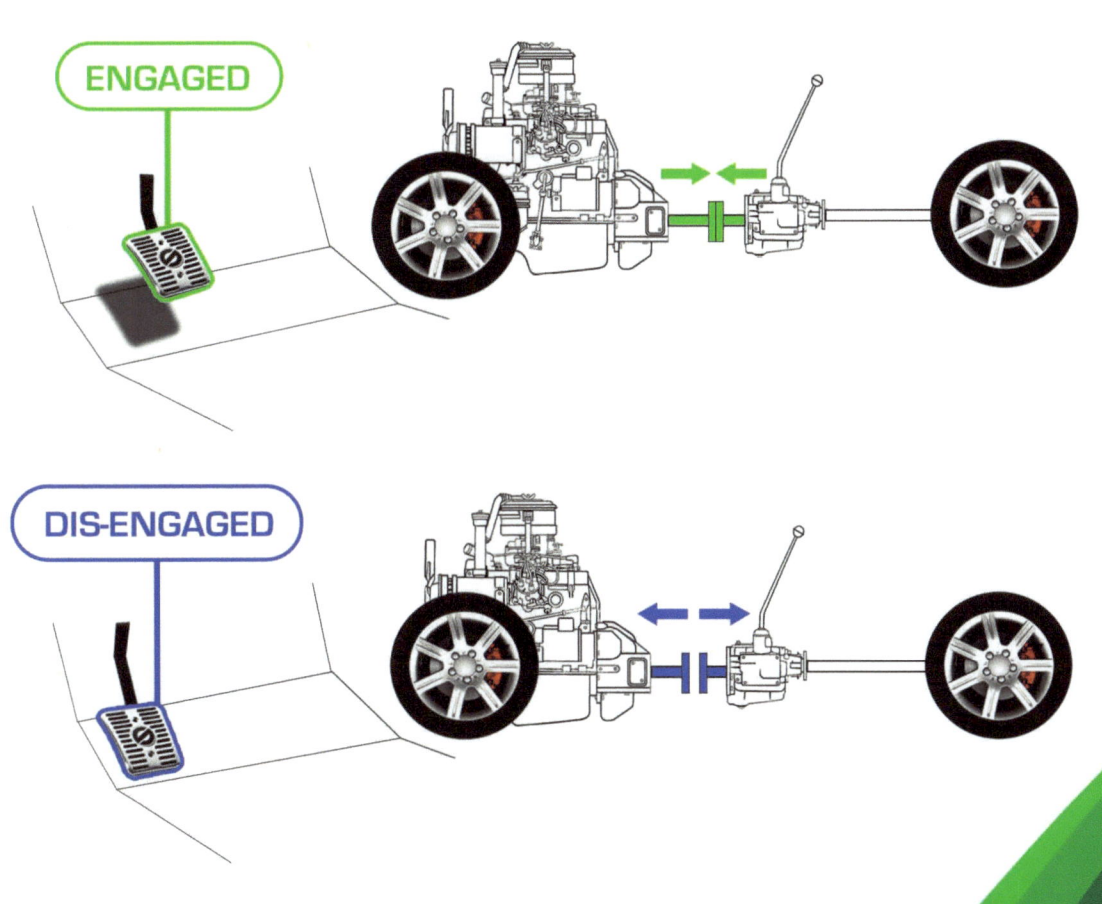

Foot Controls

Appendix 3

Because of the way the clutch works, it is only used for 3 things. They are:

. To help us **MOVE OFF**
. To control the **ENGINE** when we **STOP**,
. To **CHANGE GEAR** (that's why it is attached to the gearbox).

If we are not using the clutch for any of these 3 reasons then we should rest our foot on the **FLOOR**, away from the clutch pedal.

There are 5 positions related to the clutch, which we need to know about.
1. ENGAGED 2. RIDING 3. SLIPPING 4. 'BITE' 5. DIS-ENGAGED

Position 1 = Clutch pedal is up
Position 2 = Leaving your foot just resting against the clutch pedal (not advised because it wears out the clutch and gives you cramp in your left leg after some time stuck up in the air)
Position 3 = Used in SLOW MOVING traffic
Position 4 = Sets the clutch ready to MOVE OFF
Position 5 = Needed to CHANGE GEAR and maintain the engine when STOPPING

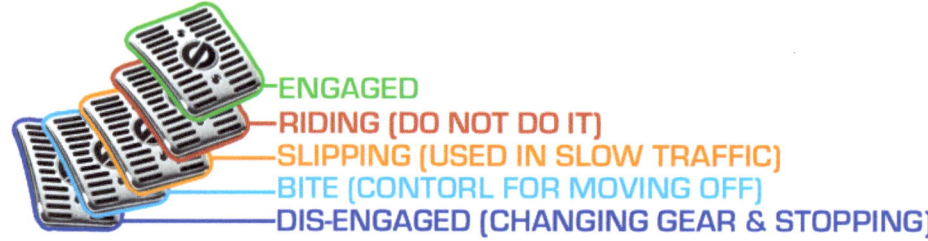

- ENGAGED
- RIDING (DO NOT DO IT)
- SLIPPING (USED IN SLOW TRAFFIC)
- BITE (CONTORL FOR MOVING OFF)
- DIS-ENGAGED (CHANGING GEAR & STOPPING)

Changing GEAR

1. OFF ACCELERATOR
2. CLUTCH TO FLOOR (DIS-ENGAGED)
3. SELECT/CHOOSE GEAR (1-5)
4. GENTLY & FULLY OFF CLUTCH
5. ONTO ACCELERATOR

Remember you only have to find your BITE when using 1st gear or when reversing!!!

Appendix 4

Now when I learnt to drive my instructor told me to use 2nd gear for left and right turns, which I duly did. Sometimes though he would tell me that I could have used 3rd gear or that I needed 1st gear at a particular turn. I could not understand why there was a difference and my instructor did not explain it to me!

The reason is that our speed and gears should MATCH each other. This, for example, means that at 3 mph we would use 1st gear and at 70 mph we would of course use 5th. That is why we use 2nd gear for left and right turns, because we should be travelling at 10-12 mph!

When you have changed gear you must release the clutch fully and take your foot away from it * Appendix 4

By doing this you will avoid two things. The first is COASTING and the second is CREEPING.

Now Coasting means that the car is in motion without being in gear i.e. you have your clutch down (dis-engaged).

Creeping means, that if you change gear TOO SOON and then drive along with you left indicator on at 10-12 mph other vehicles may think that you are intending to park on the road or even turn into premises, not be turning left at the junction ahead. If you indicated right that is just as confusing!

Clutch Control

A little exercise you might like to try to help improve your clutch control. You park on a 'slight uphill' incline. Prepare to Move Off in the usual manner (Page 16 & 17) Release your Handbrake. What happens?

1. Car rolls back
2. Nothing
3. Car moves away

Answer should be 2 – nothing because you have got the BITE! However, if your car rolls back then you did not have your BITE. So remembering our clutch adjustment from Moving Off, adjust your clutch quickly UP the £1 coin thickness then KEEP YOUR FOOT STIIL to HOLD the car in place against the gradient/incline. Then apply the Handbrake, Clutch to the floor, select Neutral and relax. Then try again. If you cannot do it, don't try more than 4 or 5 times, give the clutch a rest and try again some other time. It can take practice.

When you are able to find your BITE each time so that the car remains still, with the Handbrake off, then you are on the right track to gaining greater clutch control. Well done If you are really good you can do this WITHOUT using the Accelerator/Gas - but it isn't easy so be careful

Moving Off - Advanced

Take 3 examples - the first is a Flat Road the second is an Uphill and the third a Downhill. Question is what do you do 1st in each situation?

A. Release the Handbrake
B. Get your BITE

Answers are: Flat = A   Uphill = B   Downhill = A

So you only need to get your bite before moving off uphill otherwise you can release your Handbrake first BUT remember only release your handbrake if you will be ready to GO a split second later, so be sure about your clutch control and that it is 100% safe to go.

Imagine a ball on a flat serface, it remains still, your car, like the ball it will also remain still, so you can get your Bite after you release your Handbrake!

Downhill, you actually use your Footbrake to move away because gravity will, like it does the ball, make your car roll down the hill, so again release your handbrake first and cover your brakes!

Uphill though, you have to get the bite first, to resist gravity and prevent your car moving backwards. You may also need a little extra power from the Accelerator/Gas to help move the weight of the car up the hill!

Remember to practice moving off on all three types of road!

Appendix 6

Unit 2.1 'T' Junctions

Unit 2.2 Use of Mirrors

Unit 2.3 Correct use of Signals

Unit 2.4 Meeting Other Vehicles

Unit 2.5 Judgement of Speed
        Making Progress
        Speed Limits
        Road Positioning

Unit 3.1 Crossroads

Unit 3.2 Traffic light Sequence

Unit 3.3 Box Junctions

Unit 3.4 Vehicle Clearance

Unit 3.5 Turn in the Road
       (3Point Turn)

Coming Soon

www.ingramcontent.com/pod-product-compliance
Lightning Source LLC
Chambersburg PA
CBHW041539040426
42446CB00002B/163